THE FISHING INDUSTRY

NORTH FORELAND TO THE TWEED

Mike Smylie

AMBERLEY

Acknowledgements

Photographic books such as these are as much about the visual as the writing and therefore an author assumes the greatest gratitude to those who supplied the quality photos. Although some come from my own collection, for some of which I was behind the lens, many do not and therefore I am especially indebted to Jan Pentreath, Michael Craine, Robert Simper, Paul Arro, Edgar Readman, Shaun Clarkson, Mervyn Maggs, Don Windley, George Featherstone, The Lydia Eva & Mincarlo Trust, Paul Welch, Brian Kennell, Malcolm White and the individual members of the 40+ Fishing Boat Association for their contributions over the years. And thanks to Paul Winter for a most enjoyable trip out in his smack *Maria* and the subsequent stowboating. We were all amazed by the number of herring and sprats we caught.

General Note to Each Volume in This Series

Over the course of six volumes, this series will culminate in a complete picture of the fishing industry of Britain and Ireland and how it has changed over a period of 150 years or so, this timeframe being constrained by the early existence of photographic evidence. Although documented evidence of fishing around the coasts of these islands stretches well back into history, other than a brief overview, it is beyond the scope of these books. Furthermore the coverage of much of today's high-tech fishing is kept to a minimum. Nevertheless, I do hope that each individual volume gives an overall picture of the fishing industry of that part of the coast.

For Ana and Otis

First published 2014

Amberley Publishing
The Hill, Stroud
Gloucestershire, GL5 4EP

www.amberley-books.com

Copyright © Mike Smylie, 2014

The right of Mike Smylie to be identified as the Author of this work has been asserted in accordance with the Copyrights, Designs and Patents Act 1988.

ISBN 978 1 4456 1456 4 (print)
ISBN 978 1 4456 1470 0 (ebook)

All rights reserved. No part of this book may be reprinted or reproduced or utilised in any form or by any electronic, mechanical or other means, now known or hereafter invented, including photocopying and recording, or in any information storage or retrieval system, without the permission in writing from the Publishers.

British Library Cataloguing in Publication Data.
A catalogue record for this book is available from the British Library.

Typeset in 9.5pt on 12pt Celeste.
Typesetting by Amberley Publishing.
Printed in the UK.

Introduction

The coast in this, the fifth volume in this series, is one bordered by the North Sea, an expanse of water renowned for its freezing winds and tempestuous seas. Moreover, it is often erosion that comes to mind when the action of this sea is considered, considering the way the sea has claimed back parts of the coast in, primarily, Norfolk.

It stretches along the entire east coast of England and, with the North Sea being home to an extensive fishery up to recent times, various important fishing stations lie along its edge. It is, again, a diverse coast of river estuaries, sandy beaches, marshland and torturous cliffs.

The Hydrological Survey of 1882–9 suggested that the Thames Estuary could be considered to be that reach of sea west of a line drawn from North Foreland to Harwich in Essex, this being the extent that the estuarine sandbanks extend to. As an estuary, it is the largest in England and consists not only of the confluence of the River Thames, but that of rivers Swale and Medway in Kent and the rivers Crouch, Blackwater, Colne, Stour and Orwell in Essex, as well as their tributaries and other lesser streams. Further north of the area included in this volume are two other estuaries: the Wash and the River Humber. Other smaller rivers of consequence flow out into the North Sea at Lowestoft, Great Yarmouth, Whitby and Berwick-upon-Tweed.

In the first volume of this series we considered the herring fishery and how it affected the growth of dozens of small fishing communities along the east coast of Scotland. The same fishery improved the lot of many coastal communities along much of the coast in this volume, from the Scottish border down to East Anglia. Great Yarmouth and Lowestoft shared the centre of this great autumnal fishery which dates back to medieval times.

The smacks of the Thames estuary were renowned for their sailing ability and they undertook various fisheries that will be explained in fuller detail, principally sprats, oysters and cockles. Yorkshire fishing communities, although they were where the herring was once important, more recently have seen a growth in the lobster and crab fishery.

But most of all the North Sea is renowned for its development of the trawl fishery. It is said that Brixham boats first fished with a trawl although this isn't technically the case and the men of Barking in Essex have as much responsibility for the introduction of a fishing method that most believe has resulted in today's fishing crisis. Nevertheless, the Brixham fishers were partly responsible for the opening up of the North Sea, where huge stocks of cod and haddock were once attainable. Sadly, stocks have been overfished, though recovery does seem a realistic possibility.

Grimsby became the mother of all fishing ports, sending trawlers into the northern waters of the Atlantic, to the Faroes, Iceland and the White Sea, as well as all over the North Sea. Nearby Hull developed in a similar vein. Today, from a fishing point of view, both are redundant, Grimsby especially being a lost town with empty quays.

All in all, this is a varied coast, full of interest, with a fantastic history of fishing. It also has a fabulous history of the evolution of fishing craft, perhaps the largest collection of any of the volumes in this series.

Fishing Ways

Much has been written about the fishery of the North Sea, this being probably the richest source of fish and shellfish surrounding the British coast. Or at least it was. This capacity is largely due to the fact that the water is relatively shallow compared with many other parts of the British coast, where the continental shelf lies easily within a day's steaming of the fishing ports. Okay – so you say – but what about the Western Approaches and the Irish Sea? These were again rich in fish but of not as great an area and do not consist of vast banks interspersed with deep holes, grounds that fish just love.

Herring was indeed king here, as attested in the first volume of this series. Herring is still landed, though most goes into Scottish ports and comes from the northern reaches of the North Sea and out into the North Atlantic. The days of the Great Autumnal Fishery off East Anglia are long gone. But I've been fishing with a drift net off the mouth of the River Deben and caught a few bucketfuls. It is largely smaller fish that spawn on the sandy banks. Sprats are plentiful at times, have been and still are. Before the eighteenth century, Holland controlled most of the North Sea herring and it is said that it was the Dutch that taught the British how to fish for it!

The North Sea was responsible for the introduction of the trawl as far as Britain is concerned. The first documented evidence of trawling as such in Britain comes from 1376, when the Thames ports were petitioning to Edward III against the continued usage of a device called a *wondyrychoun*. This was likened to an oyster dredge with a closed-net mesh. A year later there came what was described as a 'machine', which consisted of a 10-foot beam with a frame at either end shaped like a 'cole rake' – the whole thing was 3 fathoms long. A sketch from 1635 shows a beam trawl affair although there is no sense of size. It has been suggested that it was a device imported from the Zuider Zee, another instance of the Dutch teaching the English and Scots how to fish.

The men of Barking, a hamlet aside a tiny creek off the Thames, had been catching herring since at least AD 670 and the hamlet was well placed to supply the London markets. Well-smacks were introduced here in 1798, and thirty-five years on there were 120 such craft based there. Twenty years later, trawling was well underway as there were 134 smacks trawling and another forty-six long-lining off the Norfolk coast.

As the power of the sail increased, so did the ability to tow trawls across the bed of the North Sea and English Channel. It is said in many circles that the small Devon village of Beer had much to do with the growth of trawling. 'Beer made Brixham, Brixham made the North Sea', the saying goes. For, even before the Barking folk were trawling the North Sea, the Brixham boats were annually joining in with the Yarmouth Herring Fair, from at least as far back as 1200.

Devon boats were travelling far and wide in their search for fish and were the protagonists in sailing across to Newfoundland for the cod fishery in the sixteenth century, where they went to search for fortunes. By 1785 there were seventy-six sailing trawlers working from Brixham, although it is said that the first men working trawling out of Brixham were Beer men in their small three-masted luggers. Some say that it was the Dutch again who taught the Brixham men to trawl. These trawlers were working the North Sea, some basing themselves for the season in Scarborough, and by the end of that century were up to almost 80 feet in length. Indeed, many Brixham skippers took their wives and families to Scarborough, where they resided at temporary homes during the fishing season while their husbands supplied the town with fish for the growing tourist trade. At the same time the smaller smacks were working over the Dogger Bank.

The story goes that it was the Brixham boats that discovered the Silver Pits in 1837. Dyson tells us how William Sudds, a Brixham fisherman who settled in Ramsgate, was master of one of several boats dispersed in a winter storm in the early winter of that year. When he limped home, his boat was said to have been staggering under the weight of fish – 2,000 pairs of sole, for which the Silver Pits became renowned. Robinson puts Sudds aboard a Margate-built smack, *Betsy*, which he first registered at Hull and then re-registered in Ramsgate in 1838. A further suggestion was made that the Silver Pits were in fact discovered in 1838 and then 'rediscovered' in 1844. Perhaps Sudds kept quiet about his discovery, took it back to Margate and then returned to the area as he was master of the 18-ton smack *Ranger* in 1844, a boat owned by J. Todd, a Hull fishmonger.

Nevertheless, trawling became the accepted method of fishing for, especially, bottom-feeding fish, although midwater trawls also fished for herring and mackerel. Dredging was another method of fishing that caused controversy because of the damage it was said to do to the seabed. The Essex and Kent smacksmen were renowned for their dredging of oysters and, as we've seen in previous volumes, they sailed far and wide in their never-ending search for rich oyster grounds.

Shellfish continue to be fished in quantity by Norfolk, Yorkshire and Northumbrian vessels. Theirs is a heritage dating back many centuries. In addition, cockle fishing has two main centres on this coast: on the Wash and around the Essex town of Leigh-on-Sea.

Shellfishing – Cockles and Oysters

Cockle sheds at Leigh-on-Sea. Leigh was an important harbour until silting of the deep water channel meant larger ships could no longer use the port. Fishing again took precedence as the town was well placed to supply the London market, helped by the arrival of the railway in 1856. Although shrimps, oysters and whitebait have been landed here in quantity, it is the cockling industry that has been the main source of shellfish for the fishermen since 1900.

Traditionally, the cockles were hand raked from the sandbanks in the Thames estuary. They were loaded on to boats which had been previously beached nearby and then, once the tide had refloated the vessel, were brought ashore to the cockling sheds, where they were cooked by steaming and the meat separated from the shell by sieving. The shells were then discarded so that the beach became a mass of shells. They were also carted away to be laid on paths and for other garden uses.

Oyster dredges being hauled by hand aboard a Whitstable oyster smack working under sail in around 1880. It is said that the Romans found oysters along this coast and sent them back to Rome. One of Britain's oldest companies, the Whitstable Oyster Company, was set up in the 1400s to farm the Royal Whitstable native oyster. The oysters are farmed over an area off Whitstable where they continue to be harvested, today with the European Protected Geographical Status.

Lobsters and Crabs

Lobsters and crabs were extensively fished on the north Norfolk coast and the fishery became centred on the towns of Cromer and Sheringham. Further north, the Yorkshire and Northumbrian coasts were also famed for their shellfish. Here, off Flamborough Head, Richard, George and Thomas Cowling are seen aboard their coble *Dawn*, H21, hauling pots. (*The Photographic Collection of Paul L. Arro*)

Pots were usually made by the fishermen, as we've seen in previous volumes. Here, George Emmerson is pictured in 1953, making a pot, watched by his two children. The pot consists of a wooden base with hoops of either metal or alkathene pipe, over which netting is fixed. The pots are usually weighted with stones or lumps of pig iron. (*The Photographic Collection of Paul L. Arro*)

Another view of pots aboard a coble, this one being the *Nancy*, H147, in 1936. Len, Tom and George Stock are hauling. The rudder of the coble lies over the stern. The construction of the pots is clearly shown and iron bars can be seen forming the longitudinal shape. Engine-driven haulers came in various guises as companies developed these labour-saving devices.

Here is a 'Highlander' hauler bringing pots up aboard the coble *Star of Hope*, WY223, in the early 1970s. As the haulers developed, the number of crews decreased accordingly so that, nowadays, potting boats as often as not are solely crewed by one man.

Salmon Fishing

Seine-netting for salmon was practised on various rivers, most notably in Northumberland and some Yorkshire estuaries. Here, the net is being hauled in as a holidaymaker looks on. Note the men are wearing waders. The boat used – a coble – can be seen beyond the men.

The River Tweed was probably the most fished river, where seine-netting for salmon was known as wear-net fishing. Here, a coble is loaded with the net prior to setting. These cobles are flat-bottomed and perhaps distant relatives of the cobles from further south. A stake net still exists at Goswick.

Stowboat Fishing

'The stowboat net and its gear were unique in elaborate complexity', according to Hervey Benham, and the device is 'a marine trap capable of trapping ten tons of fish without mechanical aid'. Benham studied the method, which involves placing a net beneath a sailing smack by means of a complicated ensemble of wooden beams, ropes and nets. The net is set over the bow of the anchored vessel and is seen here just before it is lowered into the water. It is indeed an ancient fishery which dates back to at least the fifteenth century, when it was undertaken by what were referred to as stall boats.

Here, the net is seen from ahead of the smack *Maria*, CK21, restored and belonging to Paul Winter. Again it is being set, with both wooden beams – the upper and lower baulks – visible. They are separated by a chain called the wind chain, the upper baulk being set just below the forefoot of the vessel. Lines from the ends of both baulks are attached to the anchor chain, which holds the mouth of the net open. (*Mervyn Maggs*)

11

Above: This view shows the net being hauled up after a period of two hours down. Photographed in 2012 by the author, the net was set again from the smack *Maria*, CK21. Some of the fish are caught as in a drift net, i.e. trapped by the gills.

Left: However, the bulk of the catch gathers in the cod-end of the net, in the same way that it does in a trawl net. Here the net is being lifted so that the cod-end can be brought on to the deck of the smack. However, the catch was so large that we were unable to lift it and we had to cut the net and remove some of the fish to lighten the net and subsequently lift it aboard.

Here's a close-up of the bag after we had dropped back down to remove some of the fish. The bigger fish are herring while the small ones just visible are sprats. We were fishing in the lower stretches of the River Blackwater, the largest river estuary north of the Thames. The herring here are an anadromous species, in that they swim into freshwater rivers to breed in the same way as salmon do.

Here, the fish are being sorted on the deck of the smack by the author and the vessel's owner. Stowboating used to be prosecuted by dozens of smacks out of Brightlingsea, the main port. The catch was pickled in barrels, much in the same way as herring were, and thousands of barrels were sent to Poland, Russia, Germany and Scandinavia, as well as all over Britain. Later, after the First World War, sprats were canned in vast quantities and marketed as far away as Australia. Sadly, we had a problem disposing of our monster catch, with the merchants being totally uninterested. We ate what we could, the remainder going the same way that it did in times long gone – as manure!

Herring

The typical Suffolk beach boat *Three Sisters*, IH81, is seen hauling in a drift net on the River Deben. She belongs to maritime historian Robert Simper, who bought the old boat and restored her; he often uses the boat to shoot a few nets and catch a bucketful or two of herring for home consumption. There's nothing quite like spending an early autumn morning drifting downriver and out into the North Sea, knowing that a tasty meal of fresh herring lies not too far away. (*Robert Simper*)

Another restored Simper boat is *Teddy*, IH45, a smaller typical Suffolk beach boat. Here, again, she is drifting along with a short length of drift net down. The River Deben also has a good stock of oysters and a family business has recently grown up, growing and selling fresh Deben oysters. I also remember collecting a good bucketful of cockles several years ago. (*Robert Simper*)

Right: Robert, holding the bucket, showing a few herring after a disastrous drift back in around 1990, the first time I went fishing with him. The net can be seen being hauled in over the port side.

Below: The following day we had much more success. In the white tray were a mixture of herring and sprats.

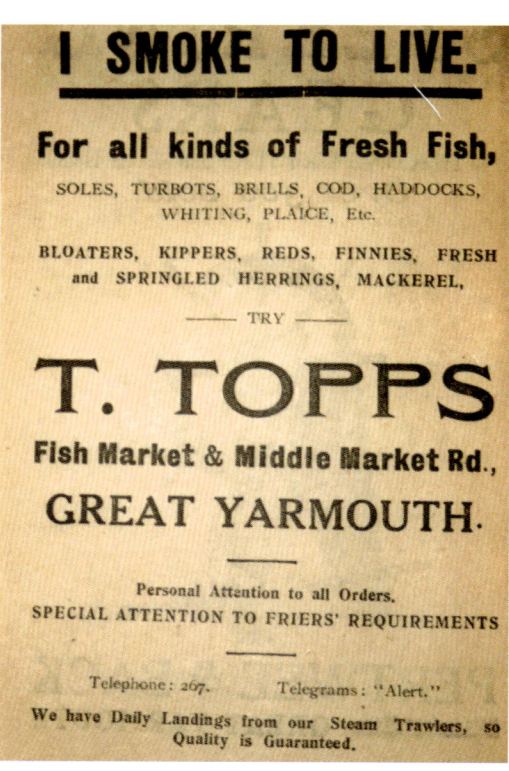

A reminder that Great Yarmouth was once a fishing port of importance, with smokehouses busy with all sorts of fish, while other species were sold fresh. Often, Great Yarmouth is regarded as being solely a herring port and this shows it was not.

It is extremely unusual to come across a smokehouse today, especially one that dates back to 1872. It was begun that year by William Fortune, in the same premises in Henrietta Street in Whitby as it uses today. Visiting it today is a real treat!

Right: Today it is run by brothers Barry and Derek, fifth-generation relations of the original William Fortune. They buy in North Atlantic herring these days, which arrive frozen, as North Sea herring is seasonal. They are then split and gutted by hand before being immersed in brine and then hung in the smokehouse and smoked for eighteen hours.

Below: Once smoked they are moved to the shop adjacent to the smokehouse, where they are sold direct to the public. A visit to Whitby is not complete without a taste of a proper fresh kipper.

Fishing Boats

Again, we have a diverse collection of fishing boats that worked these shores in the days of sail and oar. As has been said before, fishing boat design depended as much on the conditions boats had to work in as it did on the type of shore they worked from. Therefore, if a boat had to work directly from the beach, the shape was dictated by its behaviour in the type of wave that was normally encountered. This was wholly dependent on the nature of the shore, its position with regard to the prevailing wind, the slope of the beach and whether it was sandy, pebbly or rocky.

Prime examples of vessels evolving through beach use are the Cromer crab boats of north Norfolk and the cobles of Yorkshire, Durham and Northumberland. Although the craft here are similar in both counties, they pronounce it differently. Hence we have coble to rhyme with 'cobble' in Yorkshire and coble to rhyme with 'cowble' in the north. These craft, described as quintessentially English because of their development, were mentioned in the Lindisfarne Gospels and were presumably in existence well before that. That they are unique is attested by their construction. In a nutshell, a coble has a ramplank instead of a full-length keel. They were clinker-built with broad transoms, high bows and plenty of tumblehome amidships. The ramplank, by which they were measured, was typically two-thirds of the overall length and was joined to the keel, which in turn was fixed to the forefoot. The shape changed dramatically with motorisation so that the propeller was housed in a tunnel, allowing the vessel still to come ashore onto a beach.

However, the majority of fishing craft along this coast were able to shelter in the many river estuaries or in the few harbours that were built over time. Generally, the Essex smacks and bawleys sailed the Thames and its many estuaries, while Lowestoft, Yarmouth, Grimsby and Hull developed their own luggers and gaff-rigged trawlers. Suffolk had its own beach boats, as did Norfolk. More smacks emanated from the ports of the Wash – King's Lynn and Boston – while smaller individual types such as the Paull shrimper or Leigh cockle boat worked particular rivers and estuaries.

Motorisation not only affected the shape of the coble on this coast but completely changed the whole emphasis of fishing. Steam drifters and trawlers were drawn to the four main ports like flies to a carcass. As we saw in Fleetwood (volume 3), the North Atlantic fleet of trawlers soon altered in shape to suit diesel power. At the same time the traditional types – the smacks and bawleys, the cobles (as already mentioned) and the Cromer crabbers – all adapted well to motors. Although the typical motor fishing vessel worked from some of these ports, even today cobles are in the majority in the north, while around the Thames, fleets of smacks sail in their summer regattas, although they seldom actually fish any longer.

The Thames Estuary

Whitstable Oyster dredging boat at work pulling up the dredges.

Above: A Whitstable oyster smack with the crew pulling up the dredges by hand. There appear to be four dredges. The man on the after dredge is also handling the tiller to keep the vessel to wind and hove-to while the dredges are hauled. Once they have been emptied, they are then put back overboard and the vessel sails forward again.

Right: The restored Whitstable oyster smack *Emeline*, F14, built by Collars of Whitstable for the Whorlow family. She dredged for oysters in the season and then, towards the end of her working career, trawled for shrimps. She ceased fishing and was converted to a pleasure boat with a large wheelhouse in the 1950s. She then disappeared, turning up on the Costa del Sol. She eventually arrived back in Britain in 1994 and was restored in Faversham to her present state. Here she is sailing in the 2010 Swale barge match.

Two views of a Medway doble, the small inshore boats of the Kent coast, taken at Chatham in 2002. As the photographs show, there's a fish well amidships where fish can be kept alive. This well divides the boat into two and hence they became known as 'double' boats, and thence 'doble'. They are thought to have originated from the Peter boats, the traditional fishing boats of the lower reaches of the River Thames. The boats were strongly built from oak by local builders and used for harvesting smelts in winter, as well as brown shrimp trawling and oyster dredging.

Above: The bawley *Mosquito*, 144RR, in 1915. Being relatively shallow-draughted, bawleys trawled for shrimps over the sandbanks of the estuary and were commonplace at Gravesend, Leigh, Southend, Strood, Chatham, Faversham and Margate. The name 'bawley' probably comes from a corruption of 'boiler' as the installation of a boiler to cook the shrimps is the only difference between them and the large, cutter-rigged Peter boats.

Right: Here, three bawleys can be seen at Gravesend in around 1890. They have deep forefeet and long, straight keels, transom sterns and rounded hulls. The gaff sail is high-peaked and they have long topmasts with large topsails. The vessel anchored off on the left of the photograph is not a bawley but a standard local trading smack.

The bawley *Good Intent*, LO136, sailing off the Kent coast in the 1990s. Clinker-built in Faversham in 1860, she fished until 1927, was rebuilt between 1988 and 1994 and is now carvel planked. (*Don Windley*)

The bawley *Helen & Violet*, LO262, built by Cann of Harwich in 1906 for Leigh fisherman James Kimber. She fished there until the 1930s, at which time she had an engine installed and moved to Brightlingsea. After about 1972 she became a pleasure boat and has recently had a new transom and sternpost, as shown here in 2012, when she was anchored in the lower River Colne.

Right: The Leigh cockler *Mary Amelia*, LO502, built by Haywoods of Southend in 1914. Although similar in shape and rig to a bawley, she was built to load cockles off the Maplin Sands. She had an engine fitted in the 1920s and worked from Burnham-on-Crouch until the 1930s, after which she sank. Today she has been totally rebuilt and sails from the River Deben. An odd assortment of other vessels has worked the cockle beds over the years. (*Robert Simper*)

Below: The typical River Colne smack *Elise*, CK299, built by the Harris brothers at Rowhedge in the 1880s, with a party aboard for a day's fishing. She was built for spratting and trawling, and at times also dredged and trawled for shrimps. The anchor hangs over the bow while the beam trawl overhangs the counter stern.

Three Colne smacks racing in 1903. Regattas were hard-fought events among the fishing fleets all around the country and a special set of sails was often kept for this reason. Here are *Sunbeam*, CK328, *Neva*, CK86, and *Xanthe*, seen in calm waters. Smacks generally came in three sizes: the smallest, at under 35 feet, fished in the rivers and estuaries; the second class, up to 50 feet, dredged, stow-netted and trawled; while the largest, over 50 feet, dredged for oysters all over the country, sailing as far as South Wales and Luce Bay. Some fished over towards the Dutch island of Terschelling, becoming called 'skillingers' through mispronunciation!

After the Second World War, most of the smacks had been motorised and the rig had been much shortened so that a staysail could be set to steady the boat in a seaway. Here, several boats at Harwich in 1947 have their shrimp trawls hanging to dry. The smack in the foreground is the *Bluebell*, CK104, from Tollesbury. Behind are transom-sterned motor shrimpers, which became the norm in the 1950s, with wheelhouses and shallow draughts.

Right: Many smacks have survived today and can be seen keenly racing during the summer season of regattas. Here the *William & Mary*, CK32, is seen racing at the Swale barge match in 2010. Built in Gillingham, she was stored in a shed for thirty years before being bought and restored. She was eventually re-launched in 2004.

Below: The smack *Maria*, CK21, built by the Harris brothers in 1866 at Rowhedge, remains one of the oldest smacks afloat. At 47 feet, she is a mid-range vessel and the photos of stow-netting were taken aboard her in 2012. Harris' were renowned for their yachts, and *Maria* is narrower than most smacks and is fast. She has recently been restored by her owner and races, where again she is often fastest.

East Anglia and the Wash

Another smack is seen sailing well here. This is the 1885-built *Alberta*, CK318, built by Alduous of Brightlingsea. Restored between 2002 and 2004, she now sails in the various regattas around Essex.

An Aldeburgh sprat boat working with the trawl down. The rig is typical of the Suffolk beach boats – a dipping lug mainsail and small standing lug mizzen. The main difference between the dipping and standing lug is that for the latter the yard that carries the sail does not have to be lowered when tacking. For the dipping lug, the sail has to be dropped when tacking and the yard is moved around the back of the mast to be set on the other side. This, especially on the large luggers, is a lengthy process that needs a full complement of crew.

Dunwich was once an important harbour and centre of fishing until erosion saw the collapse of the port, and most of the town, into the sea after a series of storms over a century between 1286 and 1362 (according to some reports) invaded the coast. The Suffolk and Norfolk coasts are well known for their erosion due to the action of the North Sea, and houses still drop off today on occasion. The boat is a typical motorised version of the Suffolk beach boat, seen on the shingly beach by the remains of Dunwich in around 1996.

A Lowestoft trawler. These powerful gaff-rigged ketches trawled the North Sea for bottom-feeding fish. They developed from the luggers of the area that drift-netted for herring. Lowestoft trawlers were generally a bit smaller than other trawlers that worked the same grounds, though two renowned builders – Richards and Chambers – were based in the town.

The Lowestoft-registered trawler *Keewaydin*, LT1192, sailing out of the harbour in the first half of the twentieth century. She was built by Geo. & Thos Smith of Rye and launched in 1913. She fished out of Lowestoft until 1937 and, like many of the large sailing trawlers being sold off at the time to Scandinavian countries, she went to Sweden. She was renamed *Vastanvind* and registered at Lysekil, in the northern part of the Swedish west coast. During the war she worked transporting, among other things, refugees over from Nazi-held Denmark. (*Paul Welch*)

At one point, she sank after being in collision with a steamer and was raised a year later. By 1963 *Keewaydin* was in Göteborg as a yacht and then ended up in Malta until she was brought back to England in 1997. She is currently based around Falmouth and here she is seen sailing off Brixham. (*Paul Welch*)

Another Lowestoft trawler is the *Excelsior*, LT472. She was built by John Chambers of Lowestoft in 1921. She fished from the port until 1933, after which she was sold to Norway and converted to a motor coaster. She returned to England in 1971 after her owners retired and was eventually restored and is now owned by the Excelsior Trust, who operate her as a sail training vessel out of Lowestoft, from where she is sailing in the photograph.

A small Yarmouth lugger sailing out of the harbour in the 1890s. These, the forerunners of the trawlers, drifted for herring. They were previously three-masted, but they dropped the middle mast as it was found that they could drop the mainmast easily when lying to their nets. The small mizzen was left set to keep the vessel's head to wind. The bowsprit has been withdrawn on to the deck and will presumably be let out once the boat is at sea. The luggers adopted steam capstans in the 1880s, making the job of hauling in the drift net much easier.

Yarmouth was also home to a fleet of small gaff-rigged shrimpers that were kept in the harbour. These were half-deckers with a small cuddy beneath the foredeck, allowing a degree of shelter for the fishermen. Their popularity among the fishermen came about through the tourist business: the Victorians loved shrimp teas and so, at their peak in the 1880s, there were some eighty shrimpers supplying the market during the holiday period.

Left: The shrimper *Crangon*, YH55, was built in 1957, which shows that the shrimpers were still active in the second half of the twentieth century. Built with an engine, she is a bit longer and broader than the earlier sailing versions. Here, she is seen with her shrimp trawl hanging over the stern in the River Deben, after a trawl downriver which resulted in a bucketful of shrimps and some small flatties. *Crangon* is now currently owned in Holland.

Below: Cromer is famous for its crabs and here is one such typical north Norfolk crab boat. These craft, evolving from craft across the North Sea, have probably worked this coast since the days of the Viking landings in the eighth century as some writers suggest a Saxon influence. Nevertheless, crabbing was most definitely the main preoccupation for Cromer fishers, as in 1875 there were 120 of them among a population of 1,145. The boats sailed with a single dipping lugsail and the holes in the upper strake, called 'orrucks', were to pass oars through to enable the men to carry the boat ashore.

Three Views of a Cromer Boat Coming Ashore by Tractor

Motorisation affected the shape of these boats, as it did everywhere. It had the added effect of allowing tractors to pull vessels up the beach. The flat-bottomed boat is left in the shallow water, tended by a crew member, the bow facing seaward.

The tractor reverses the trailer to the boat, the tow rope is connected to the sternpost, and hauling on to the trailer begins.

Once safely on the trailer, tractor and boat can be taken up the beach to await the next launch.

Above: A postcard view of Cromer with the crab boats all lined up on their trailers. Today, however, the majority of the boats are fibreglass copies, although a wooden version of the Cromer crab boat has only recently been built (2014).

Left: A clinker-built Lynn yoll lies in a small pill. The word 'yoll', coming from the Norse *yol*, meaning small boat, betrays the boat's ancestors: the Norsemen. These double-enders were similar in shape to the north Norfolk punts but adopted the cutter rig for being handy around the channels of the Wash, where they were used for shrimping, cockling and musselling. Some boiled their shrimp catch aboard. They were flat enough in the floors to sit upright when collecting shellfish from the sandbanks. Most of the Lynn yolls were built by Thomas Worfolk or his sons at their King's Lynn yard.

A Yarmouth-registered yoll dried out at Blakeney. The shape here is beamer than the previous photograph and shows a likeness to the Cromer crab boats. In reality there often isn't much difference in local craft, even though modern man has given them different names. Terminology is often the science of the academic – the fishermen just called them all punts!

The Wash was also home to the Wash smack, which was used mostly for shrimping. Here the Wash smack *Privateer* is sailing in the Swale barge match in 2010. She was built by Gostelow of Boston. These boats are smaller than the Essex smacks and worked two trawls – one 8 feet forward and another 12 feet aft – in the waters of the Boston deeps.

On the estuary of the River Humber, lower down but on the outskirts of Hull, was the small village of Paull, where a small fleet of shrimpers were based. These cutter-rigged boats worked the Lincolnshire side of the river between March and September and it is said that they worked the same way as they had done since the fourteenth century, with ancient beam trawls. By 1901 there were only twenty boats left and the last boat, *Venture*, seen here, ceased fishing in 1950.

33

The Coble Coast

The coble, as described earlier, is probably the most recognisable of the small inshore craft because of its extraordinary shape. Here the *Lily*, WY135, is sailing up the river at Whitby with a reef in the sail. She represents the typical inshore coble used for all manner of fishing, from trawling and long-lining to potting for lobsters and crabs. She has no foresail. (*Edgar Readman*)

On the other hand, the larger coble *Gratitude*, WY97, is seen sailing with foresail on a bowsprit. She was the last boat built by Hector Handyside at Harrison's Yard in Amble. (*George Featherstone*)

A seemingly peaceful scene with a larger coble sailing in Scarborough harbour. By contrast, some motor keelboats are moored up on the left-hand side of the photograph. (*Edgar Readman*)

Although cobles are often regarded as the only inshore boats working the north-east coast, mules were considered half-breed boats. Initially there were double-ended cobles that had evolved from direct Viking influence but others regard them as a Scottish influence and say that they are combinations of cobles and whaling boats. Keelboats are different, although they appear similar in shape. Here the mule *Dora Ann* is seen at Scarborough in around 1900.

Two keelboats on the slip at Scarborough in 1999. Both were motorised and were used for potting.

Over ten years later, I took this photograph in Scarborough in almost the same place. Here two cobles sit on the slip. The one on the right appeared almost redundant while the other was clearly used for fishing. However, the angle does give a great view of the bottom of this craft and of the bilge keels, called 'draughts' ('skorvels' in Northumberland).

The coble *Northern Star*, SH139, being recovered from the sea at Filey in 1987. Note that the tractor is pulling the trolley itself and not the boat, as was the case in Cromer. The full body of the motor coble is obvious in the photo. (*Paul L. Arro*)

A lovely view of the coble *RFN*, WY50, on its trailer at Skinningrove, a small village by a stream between Staithes and Saltburn. The hauler suggests the vessel is used for potting, judging by the hull protection. However, it would appear that the boat hasn't been used for some time. Although a fishing station, the village developed in the mid-1850s from the export of iron and steel from the steelworks. By the 1970s it was just the refuge of some cobles once again. (*Mike Craine*)

A coble on the Landing at Filey. Filey was once a major fishing station and in 1866 there were sixty-four cobles working from here. The bay is relatively sheltered by Filey Brigg, though it has recently suffered from flash floods. The cobles always seem to attract the attention of holidaymakers, especially when launching and beaching.

The coble *Lead Us*, BH87, entering Beadnell harbour in 2001. The protective canvas over the forward portion of the boat is often seen in Northumberland cobles. It offers a degree of shelter beneath.

Owned by the Bridlington Sailing Coble Preservation Society, in 2012 this boat was surveyed and found to be in need of serious attention. Since then, boatbuilder John Clarkson, along with Joe Gelsthorpe, has almost rebuilt the boat and she was launched again in March 2013; she is seen here sailing soon after. (*Paul L. Arro*)

The deck view of the Bridlington coble *Three Brothers* in around 2010. She was built by Percy and Baker Siddall of Bridlington in 1912. At 40 feet she is a large coble, the last one at Bridlington, although the company built several, as did Arg Hopwood of Flamborough. In the summer, many of these were packed with holidaymakers having a trip out around the bay.

The Effect of Steam and the Internal Combustion Engine

The first impact of steam was that steamers were used to tow sailing boats out of harbour, often in trots of several craft. Here at Lowestoft, several sailing trawlers are being hauled out towards the sea by the paddle steamer *Imperial*.

Various photographs of the fish market quay at Lowestoft, showing a variety of steam drifters. The market hall can be seen in most of the shots – it is the long, low building alongside the quay. Boats would almost fight for space to nose in to the quay to unload their herring.

Huge amounts of herring passed through this market. In 1913, at the peak of the industry, some 536,400 crans of herring passed through (a cran being about 1,000 fish), only surpassed by Yarmouth with 824, 213 crans. (*All courtesy of Jan Pentreath*)

A typical steam drifter retained the mizzen sail to hold the vessel to wind while lying to the drift nets. The engine was below the casing behind the wheelhouse. These boats were nicknamed 'Pipe-stalkies' because of the high smoking funnel. The accommodation was forward and was renowned as being uncomfortable in a seaway as the bow would lift and then drop several feet off a wave. Inside, things were left mid-air, and its effect on the human body was not particularly pleasant!

The steam drifter/trawler *Lydia Eva*, YH89, is the best preserved of these vessels today. After a recent lottery grant, she has had much work done to her iron hull and steam engine. She is based in Great Yarmouth but also sails out of nearby Lowestoft in the summer. She was built in King's Lynn and launched in 1930, at a time when the industry was contracting. She only fished for nine years before being sold and used in a variety of ways until being laid up in 1969. Today, she belongs to the Lydia Eva & Mincarlo Charitable Trust. (*The Lydia Eva & Mincarlo Charitable Trust*)

The Trust also owns the *Mincarlo*, LT412. Built by the Brooke Marine yard in Lowestoft, she was launched in 1961 as a side trawler, known as a sidewinder because of this. Named after an island in the Scillies by her owners, W. H. Podd Ltd, as were her two sister vessels, *Bryher* and *Rosevear*, she only fished for thirteen years. However in that time she was always among the top landers, bringing in cod, plaice, haddock, skate and sole. In the 1990s she was bought by the Trust and opened to the public in Lowestoft in 1998.

Leaving Lowestoft: two steam drifters sail alongside a diesel motor trawler as they set out to their respective fishing grounds. The difference between the two types is stark.

Two Grimsby steam trawlers tied up. On the left is *War Duke*, GY1037, launched in 1917. Alongside her is *Varanis*, GY511, built in 1909. Above her is the coal shoot, and the hoist is swinging to load her up with coal. The picture was taken in the 1920s.

The Hull-registered *Banyers*, H255, leaving harbour. Built by Cook, Welton & Gemmell in 1939 as the *St Zeno*, H255, she was renamed in 1952 and scrapped in Belgium in 1966. During the war she was requisitioned for submarine duties only a month after her launch in 1940 and remained in naval service until 1946. For a while in 1942 she was loaned to the US Navy, albeit with a Royal Navy crew aboard.

The Grimsby-registered sidewinder *Ross Cheetah*, GY614, one of several boats owned by Ross Trawlers Ltd and called 'cat class' vessels. One, the *Ross Tiger*, GY318, survives as a permanent memorial to the fishermen of Grimby, berthed outside the National Fishing Heritage Centre in Grimsby.

Another view of *Ross Cheetah* at Buckie. She was built in 1959 by Cochranes of Selby and was the sixth. *Ross Tiger* was first, followed by *Ross Leopard, Ross Jaguar, Ross Panther* and *Ross Cougar*. Then came *Ross Lynx, Ross Jackal, Ross Puma, Ross Genet, Ross Civet* and finally *Ross Zebra*, though it might be noticed that two of these latter vessels are not big cats! *Ross Cheetah* was sold to Spain in 2000.

Motor Fishing Vessels

MFVs are simply lovely craft and I include this photo as it is one of my favourites. The boats are *Ajax*, IH107; *Gleaners*, WK325; one registered IH205; and behind one registered RX for Rye, port of Sussex. The photo was taken in an Essex/Suffolk river, though by 1968 only one vessel was registered at Ipswich.

The Scottish-built seine-net boat *Triumph*, GY467, entering the Fish Dock basin at Grimsby in 1959. (*John Firth/Creative Commons*)

The ring-netter *June Rose*, LH205, built by Weatherheads of Cockenzie in 1937 for the Clarke family of Musselburgh/Fisherrow, seen here in Whitby.

But it wasn't just ring-net boats from the east of Scotland that came to Whitby for the herring season there. Here are several Clyde ringers moored up at Whitby. The boat in the foreground, *Maireared*, BA196, was built in 1932, by Weatherheads of Cockenzie again, and fished out of The Maidens and then Tarbert. She worked until 1964 then was converted into a pleasure boat and is still sailing. Her original Gardner 4L3 engine is still in her and was the very first of these L3 engines.

Another view of Whitby, showing the extent of the boats moored up during the herring season. Many would be Scottish vessels.

Various Scottish-built seine-net boats moored up at Bridlington. Two are registered in Grimsby, one in Hull and one in Scarborough. On the inside of the near trot is a steam drifter. The photograph seems to have been taken soon after the Second World War.

Three boats at Scarborough. Left to right: *Pioneer*, LH397; *Jann Denise*, FR80; and *Clara Gwynne*, SN6. These wooden fishing boats date from the 1970s. (*Mike Craine*)

In contrast, these are boats of a more modern era: *Elvina*, SH129; *Magic*; *Cornucopia*, OB7; and *Gannet*, PD989. I can't imagine that these will cause an outcry when they come to the end of their working lives. (*Mike Craine*)

A Danish type of boat at Sunderland. *Des*, GY582, was built in Denmark in 1943 on the same lines as hundreds of other seine-net boats. Ports such as Esbjerg were full of them, with their great one-cylinder engines with their telltale sound. When they started working the western side of the North Sea and landing into Grimsby, they became known as 'snibbies' and many were brought into the British fleet.

Vendelbo, GY734, was again built in Denmark, but in 1957, and represents the last of these snibbies. The stempost is almost straight and the stern is less of a canoe stern and more of a cruiser stern. The wheelhouse is steel and larger, and there is a power block at the after end for hauling in.

As a reminder that modernisation has affected the fishing fleets throughout Britain, here is a fibreglass vessel dating from 2000. Based in Seahouses, *Standsure*, BK552, is working pots off the Farne Islands in 2013. (*Paul L. Arro*)

50

Fishing Folk

Whereas fishing methods and fishing boats are the tools of the fishermen, it is the social history of the fisherfolk themselves that in some ways is the true story of fishing. These fishers survived in their insular communities strung out all along the coasts of eastern England and the various rivers of the south-east; each had their own traditions and ways of living and fishing. Not until twentieth-century fishing displaced these communities in favour of large ports did they change: they had remained constant over generations until then. Son followed father who had followed grandfather into fishing – there was generally no other choice.

Throughout much of Britain, fishing communities tended to be separate from the general populace, often set aside at the end of the town. Often these communities weren't just about fishing, and boatbuilding was an equally important part of the story. The boats had to be built and the east coast was home to several itinerant boatbuilders who would travel to a particular settlement to build a boat for some individual. Boatbuilding yards – or more likely available waterside fields – spread in the nineteenth century so that a whole host of builders were producing small boats for the local fishers. Sailmakers and blacksmiths contributed, as did the various net-makers. Once the fish were landed, they had to be sent straight to market, hawked about the locality or processed. Processing usually involved either a salt-cure or a smoke-cure until the advent of refrigeration, deep-freezing and processes such as fish-finger production. Grimsby, with its fleet of boats, the largest in the world at one time, had all sorts of fish-processing factories serving the world.

From Boat to Market

Here a coble, *Gratitude*, has just come ashore at Robin Hood's Bay. The dog seems to be the only one looking at the camera! Coble fishing out of the cliff-hugging village has been immortalised in the Bramblewick Trilogy by local writer Leo Walmsley (*Three Fevers*, *Sally Lunn* and *Phantom Lobster* – first published by Collins in 1932). (*Edgar Readman*)

In this image the fishermen are again bringing the catch ashore. Here at the North Landing, Flamborough, they have a donkey poised to carry the heavy load up the steep hill. The basket is a typical quarter-cran. (*Paul L. Arro*)

Again at the North Landing, the men are preparing to pull the boats up, away from the ravishes of the sea. The man on the right is possibly dragging baulks of timber to slide the boats up on. (*The postcard collection of Paul L. Arro*)

The coble *Skip*, SN23, coming back onto the Coble Landing at Filey in 1987. Tractors have replaced manual labour to a certain extent. (*Paul L. Arro*)

An informal fish market at Whitby. The women are selling the catch that their husbands and/or sons have brought in that morning. Sometimes this was hawked about the locality.

The life of the trawlerman was hard. Here, the net is about to come aboard.

A heap of fish in the Lowestoft fish market. This looks to be chiefly herring and would be sold off, barrelled up and sent off to a curer within hours of being landed. Only something like a quarter of herring landed would be eaten fresh, the rest being cured either in salt or smoke.

A typical quayside scene after the boats had discharged their fish. Ice still lies around, though the market hall seems quite full. Presumably the auction has begun. This was repeated daily throughout the season except for Sundays.

55

Here fresh herring is being packed in salt in wooden boxes, a process known as 'klondykeing'. Most of this herring was sent to Germany until the outbreak of war in 1914. The process was nowhere near as exacting as barrelling the herring in the Scotch Cure process.

Here at Great Yarmouth, herring is being loaded straight into withy baskets known as 'swills' in East Anglia. These would be sold as seen and carried away for the baskets to be emptied.

A close-up of a swill on exhibition aboard the steam drifter/trawler *Lydia Eva* in 2010. These were unique to East Anglia.

Here herring is being unloaded from a Yorkshire yawl at Whitby. The boats are half-deckers and the fish hold amidships is literally full of herring. It seems to be being put into baskets and carried over another boat to the quay, a laborious job indeed.

Two views of a pile of herring on the quay at Whitby prior to it being barrelled. The fleet anchored off seems to have Scottish boats among it and most of these vessels are ring-netters. It certainly has attracted a large crowd.

The Herring Lassies

Here is a group of Scotch girls at the gutting trough (the farlane) at Hartlepool. Anywhere along the east coast where fish could be landed saw some degree of herring curing.

A similar scene at Scarborough and it certainly must have been a smelly, filthy job! Nevertheless, the herring lassies were known as a jolly bunch of hard workers.

Sometimes the herring were cured in curing yards and sometimes on the quay where they were landed, as in this case. However, this photograph must have been taken at the end of the day as the farlane is almost empty and only four women remain at work.

Here the gutting seems to be taking place in a street of houses. The barrels are being topped up with brine after the herring have been allowed to cure for a couple of days.

This view shows the extent of gutting in Lowestoft. The barrels are five high and the farlane at least 30 feet in length, probably longer. The women's backs must have been made of steel!

A poignant photo of a woman concentrating on her work. Taken in Lowestoft in the 1930s, the woman is packing a barrel of herring. The fish had to be laid the correct way up, in alternative layers, to ensure maximum capacity.

Stoking the boiler on the *Lydia Eva* in 2012. These boats needed tons of coal to keep at sea.

Above left: Boatbuilder Fred Crowell of South Shields caulking the deck of a boat. Even though boatbuilders are few and far between along this coast, there are still several from Kent to Berwick capable of rebuilding anything from a Thames sailing barge to a coble.

Above right: An advert for all sorts of nets, a reminder that different fisheries needed different nets.

Boats Built by Billy Clarkson of Whitby

Above: The inside of Billy's workshop at Dock End, Whitby. Billy started his working life at fourteen, at Whitehall shipyard in Whitby, as his father was foreman. After about a year, both father and son left to start their own business, W. Clarkson & Sons. This is where, under his father's guidance, Billy completed his six-year apprenticeship in boatbuilding. Billy's other brothers, Charlie, David and Paul, also helped out at the family business, and later so did his son Peter. (*Shaun Clarkson*)

Right: Billy's father, William Clarkson, was already very well known in coble building, as in the 1930s he was the inventor of the 'Streamed Tunnel' or 'Raised Ram Tunnel'. The Streamed Tunnel is constructed when building motorised cobles. Before this, coble builders would build the bottom of the coble, between the drafts the natural curve, then cut out the planks and fit a 'Box' over it to accommodate the propeller and protect it. This was known as a 'Box Tunnel'. The picture on the right shows how the floor of the coble looks with a Streamed Tunnel. Billy is standing in the coble. (*Shaun Clarkson*)

Billy Clarkson's first coble, *Golden Crown*, WY78, on launch day. Although the *Golden Crown* was built by Billy, he never saw the launch as he was completing his national service in the Army at the time. (*Shaun Clarkson*)

The *Golden Crown* after being taken down to the water's edge. She was built in 1953 for Richard, Matthew and Francis Verrill of Staithes and was powered by a Petter 10 hp two-cylinder diesel engine. (*Shaun Clarkson*)

The *Golden Crown* being launched down the embankment straight into the river. The passers-by on the coach had a bird's-eye view! (*Shaun Clarkson*)

Remembrance, WY138, was built by Billy for Ralph Tose in 1959. (*Shaun Clarkson*)

The coble *Mabel*, SH168, being lifted into the water. The drafts or bilge keels are clearly seen, with quite an amount of curvature. *Mabel* was built in 1965 for Ken Leader, who fished with her from Scarborough (SH). (*Shaun Clarkson*)

Above: Mabel in the river at Whitby soon after launch. In the background is the *Provider*, KY201, built by Millers of St Monans. (*Shaun Clarkson*)

Left: The *Renown*, WY71, built by Billy and his nephew David Clarkson in Billy's yard in 1972. The boat was for John's own use at Bridlington, where he later moved to work on his own account. (*Shaun Clarkson*)

Along the Coast

The many tributaries of the River Thames, and the muddy creeks off them, play host to numerous places where boats of all sizes can either dry out on the ebb or remain afloat throughout the tide. Furthermore there are, of course, the various ports and harbours, some commercial and others not.

Away from the estuary and north of the rivers of Suffolk that again provide plenty of shelter, there are the ports which have grown up at river mouths, Lowestoft and Great Yarmouth being prime examples. The North Norfolk coast, sandy and backed by dunes, has several indents while Sheringham and Cromer are, to some extent, exposed to the North Sea. The Wash, too, provides shelter and several ports upstream of the few rivers that flow into it, i.e. King's Lynn and Boston.

The River Humber affords shelter to both Grimsby and Hull, the former coming to the forefront of the British fishing industry in the mid-nineteenth century. Hull, a few miles upstream, probably declined from a fishing point of view as Grimsby grew though it remained a significant fish port. It was an important whaling station until the emphasis shifted to trawling. Like Grimsby, the Cod Wars saw an end to the fishing industry in Hull.

The Yorkshire coast has a number of small bays and inlets with a vibrant fishing industry, and several ports such as Bridlington and Scarborough. Places like Robin Hood's Bay, Runswick Bay and Staithes have associations with smuggling at the same time. Hartlepool, Sunderland and North Shields have fishing associations.

The Northumberland coast has been described as England's unspoilt secret and is a most glorious adventure for any coastal traveller. Fine beaches, small rivers and some fine heritage combine with fishing history at every turn. And then we are back at Berwick, where we started five volumes ago!

Small whelk boats at Whitstable in around 1910. This fishery was dominated by Norfolk families, and the design of these double-enders certainly shows a resemblance to the north Norfolk crab boats.

Fishing today in Whitstable is very different, as elsewhere. Here, two trawlers lie alongside in 1998.

Above: Faversham's muddy creek berths provide a place for redundant fishing boats to relax. Note the dry dock, where boats can dry out for painting and general overhaul.

Right: Faversham creek in 2010. The boat under cover is the converted Danish fishing vessel *Willow*, while across the creek is Standard Quay, until recently a haven for many vessels including Thames sailing barges. Under the white tent is the barge *Cambria*, restored to full sailing state with the help of lottery money. However, the quay has recently been bought by a property developer and most of the boats have, it appears, been forced elsewhere.

The cockle sheds at Leigh-on-Sea. This shed seems to be selling everything from a houseboat to an anchor for it, as well as cockles!

The Strand at Leigh, proving that there was more to the town than cockles. Here, a Victorian gentleman's yacht is drawn up the town slipway for some needy work.

The river at Leigh in 1996. The boats still go out cockling and the beach is still a mass of shells, but there is today some semblance of order in Leigh.

The Essex smack *Hyacinth* being launched in May 1997 in Maldon, Essex, after a rebuild by local boatbuilders Brian Kennell and Shaun White. (*Brian Kennell*)

The 1964-built Scottish boat *Forethought*, CK194, at West Mersea in 2010. West Mersea is renowned for its oyster fishery but this boat shows that some trawling, mostly for shrimps, occurs in the area.

Nearby Brightlingsea is a haven for smacks, some seen here in their winter protection in the mud of the Colne Smack Preservation Society dock. This was the site of the Aldous boatbuilding yard, which was one of the most productive of the yards building smacks in the nineteenth and early twentieth centuries.

Above: Two Yarmouth shrimpers at the Sail Ipswich Festival in 1997. *Horace & Hannah*, the nearest, was built in 1906 and is the oldest of these craft. Alongside is the 1957-built *Crangon*.

Left: The crew of *Crangon* shooting a drift net on the River Deben. Shrimpers weren't usually for catching herring but on this occasion we were experimenting!

The beach at Aldeburgh with tripping boats and a couple of beach huts in the sea. The boat on the right is a typical two-masted Suffolk beach boat.

Dunwich beach looking north in 1997. Several boats still worked from the beach. The baulks of timber lying in front of the boats are to ease their passage into the sea. Although Suffolk beach boats, these are purely built for motors and are much fatter in the body to cope with the extra buoyancy needed to counter the weight of the engine.

Southwold beach in the late nineteenth century. As in Aldeburgh, the fishermen make more of a living running trips around the bay with the holidaymakers, as well as renting out bathing huts, than they do from fishing. Out of season they return to fishing.

73

The fleet leaves Lowestoft in a calm sunset. These boats would only stay out for a day or two before returning with their catch, as the fishing grounds were seldom more than a few hours away from the coast.

Lowestoft herring basin crowded with vessels. However, it is obviously outside the herring season as the majority of these boats are ketch-rigged sailing trawlers. At least three are registered in Ramsgate. The fish market is on the far side of the basin.

The fish market at the height of the herring industry in the early twentieth century, with steam drifters vying for a place at the quay to unload. (*Malcolm White*)

Lowestoft again in the herring season. Here, the barrel yards belonging to the various curers are stacked high with barrels that have either been filled or will be transported to where the herring lassies are curing the fish.

A similar scene in nearby Great Yarmouth. The boat on the left is registered at Buckie on the Moray Firth. Hundreds of Scottish boats followed the herring southwards and ended up at either Yarmouth or Lowestoft.

More Scottish drifters of a later date at Great Yarmouth. These boats, up to 80 feet in length, were superb catching machines and represented the peak of Scottish fishing-boat building.

Two Cromer crab boats on their trailers. These are motorised vessels and hence fuller bodied than the sailing boats, and the 'orrucks' have disappeared as they are no longer carried up the beach.

The same beach looking the other way, eastwards, where several other boats lie on the sand. This was taken in around 1996. Today the majority of the fleet are fibreglass craft.

The beach at East Runton in around 1880. Several crab boats lie in the shelter of the dunes. These boats were common all along the north Norfolk coast.

77

East Runton several decades later. Again, the crabbers are motorised and kept ashore on trailers. Nevertheless, today there are no working boats here.

Blakeney, west of Sheringham and Cromer, was an important port in the Middle Ages, as was nearby Cley-next-the-Sea. With silting, the harbour was dredged in the early nineteenth century but continuing silting, and the advent of larger vessels, meant it lost its trade. Fishing was only practised on a small scale and today it is a haunt of tourists and weekend cottage owners.

The fishing fleet in the Fisher Fleet, as the dock is called, at King's Lynn in around 1998. Most were shrimpers working the channels of the Wash.

The Fisher Fleet from the other end, showing the boats with their nets drying. The beam trawls can be seen on the port side of the two vessels in the foreground.

The Scottish ring-net boat *Kingfisher* seen in the river at Boston in 1995. By this time she had been converted for pleasure. The shrimp net belongs to a small boat alongside.

An aerial view of the docks at Grimsby. The Dock Tower at the entrance to the Royal Dock was built in 1851 and the Fish Dock five years later. The large Fish Dock No 2 came in 1877 when a new entrance was built, along with a large fish market.

Grimsby Fish Dock at the height of the steam trawler days. The Dock Tower is again easily recognisable and could be seen from miles way. It was often the first and last landmark fishermen saw during their weeks away at sea.

Hull-registered boats at Bridlington in the 1930s. Left to right: *Boys Own*, H205; *Wayside Flower*, H117; *Forward*, H433; *Excelsior*, H97. The boats are unusual in that they are double-enders (probably brought from Scotland) and have a centre and forward mast.

81

The North Landing at Flamborough, which was home to the majority of the Flamborough fishing fleet, although there's also a more exposed South Landing on the other side of Flamborough Head. Although it's a steeply sloping landing, there were numerous cobles based there at one time. (*Paul L. Arro*)

The North Landing in 1995, with several motorised cobles.

The North Landing in 2010 on a calmer day. Even if the fishing industry is contracting, there will always be a few craft working from beach-based communities such as this.

Bridlington harbour with sailing cobles moored up.

Bridlington harbour with a fleet of cobles leaving with trippers aboard. Presumably this is some sort of fête day as there are crowds gathered all around the harbour, and such a fleet leaving at the same time would be extraordinary.

Another view of Bridlington with a sailing coble leaving the harbour, again with crowds of people lining the quays. The main fleet is moored up. All Bridlington cobles were painted in a pale blue or white colour.

Cobles and a mule on the beach at Filey in around 1880. (*Edgar Readman*)

The Coble Landing at Filey, crowded with motorised cobles, in 1979. Although then fishing was more prevalent than today, the Landing is still home to a fair few cobles. (*Paul L. Arro*)

85

Scarborough, with a mixture of vessels alongside the outer side of the Fish Quay. The boat registered as NN66 is from Newhaven in Sussex. Alongside that boat is an early steamer. The quayside is crowded with visitors, locals and barrels.

Scarborough again, with vessels alongside the Outer Pier, and the lighthouse marking the entrance and end of the Old Pier. The two nearest boats appear to be trading ketches while there's a Scarborough-registered ketch beyond.

Two colourful photos of Scarborough in the 1950s with Scottish boats in the harbour.

Whitby harbour, with an old coble alongside one of the Yorkshire yawl boats that fished for herring primarily. In 1860 there were 100 such vessels working the Yorkshire coast, including twelve in Whitby. Filey had the highest number at thirty. They were flat-bottomed for beaching and were generally laid up out of the herring season. A new one cost about £600 at that time.

A photo taken in roughly the same place, though slightly downriver. The white house can be seen on the left of the last photo, unpainted. However, another yawl lies laid up while there's a good fleet of cobles.

Children playing around in the water near the entrance to Whitby harbour with a coble in attendance. It would appear the baskets are for catching something.

Cobles at Runswick Bay in 2010. *J. T. Gannet* is fibreglass.

Port Mulgrave was a loading place for the Palmer Iron Company to ship out ironstone to its furnaces on the River Tyne until its closure in 1916. Today, it is a haven for various boats of differing states as well as a few fishermen's huts. Most of the harbour has long gone.

Staithes is a picturesque village straddling a small stream and is known as being the birthplace of Captain Cook. It was also once home to a considerable fishing fleet. It has an outer harbour enclosed by two breakwaters.

In around 1995 there were still various boats in the river, this photograph showing a mixture of cobles and keelboats at low water.

Then, on a visit in 2010, these were the only two vessels there. Is this a sign of the times?

Sunderland harbour with steam drifters alongside. Sunderland is rarely thought of as a fishing harbour and was developed purely to export coal.

However, there was a substantial fish market in the early twentieth century. Nowadays that has gone, although there remains a fishmonger's on the old fish quay.

The small creel boat *Marean*, KY120, in Fred Crowell's boatyard at South Shields in 2001. Built by Millers of St Monans in 1949, she fished until around 2000, when she changed hands. When she emerged from the shed, she was rigged with two lugsails. (*A. R. van Hee*)

Craster men posing around the capstan at the top of the old slip where boats were once hauled up. Although regarded as a fishing community, Craster's harbour was built largely to export stone from the nearby quarry. Capstans were vital among small fishing communities to haul up their craft.

Three cobles on the beach at Craster. Craster is also home to the Robson smokehouse business; their kippers are widely renowned and available in supermarkets such as Waitrose.

Abandoned boats on Holy Island. Although several potting boats work from the island, these boats were once used to seine-net for salmon. The black shapes are upturned boats.

Two more upturned fishing boats at Holy Island, used as fishermen's huts. One was vandalised several years ago and, so important are they from a heritage point of view, the Heritage Lottery allocated a grant for its rebuilding.

Two boats of contrasting shape: the Seahouses-built *Children's Friend*, BK157, dates from 1963 while the coble *Remembrance*, BK199, was built in Amble in 1964. Same building era but of a wholly different ancestry, which makes this coast most interesting.

And, as a final reminder that we have completed the circumnavigation of mainland Britain, we come to the *Coral Isle*, SN22, which was built in Berwick. This was the first of twenty-three sidewinders, nicknamed 'Sputniks' or 'Rocket trawlers', and was launched in 1956 for J. Rutherford of North Shields. These Fair Isle Class trawlers, designed by M. Gueroult and adapted by Fairmile, were built over several years after Fairmile had taken over the Berwick shipyard from Weatherheads in 1953. After the Fair Isle class, Fairmile produced the Croan class after 1969. Fairmile sold the yard in 1973 and shipbuilding did recommence for a short while over the next few years though it finally came to an end in 1979.